If my thoughts could speak

Sanvi Bhandari

BookLeaf Publishing

India | USA | UK

Made with ❤ on the BookLeaf Publishing Platform
www.bookleafpub.in
www.bookleafpub.com

Dedication

To my parents, my sister and Dada,

For always, always believing in me.

Preface

If My Thoughts Could Speak is a landscape of the soul, where words are woven into an escapade for every wanderer seeking a taste of life. This collection of poetry represents a tapestry of emotions, experiences, and reflections, each thread intricately beaded into this piece.

Within these pages, you will find echoes of joy, whispers of sorrow, and the delicate balance between the two. Each poem is a fragment of a larger whole—a glimpse into a world where everything may seem disparate, yet through these verses, I hope to reveal the invisible threads that binds us. The verses explore themes of love, loss, hope, and care, offering both a mirror to our shared humanity and a window into our individuality.

Poetry has always been a sanctuary for those seeking to understand the unspoken— a vessel for the intangible. Through these poems, I invite you to ponder, reflect, and connect with the profound beauty that lies within the most overlooked moments of life. These words are not merely an expression of my own journey but a universal dialogue— one that speak to anyone who has ever found solace in creativity, a refuge for the crazy and people who live outside the box.

As you turn these pages, I hope you discover something of yourself within the verses. Let each poem resonate with you, stirring emotions and thoughts that may have been patiently waiting for their moment to surface. Poetry is a dance between the writer and the reader—so here's to our first dance, and many more to come...

Thank you for allowing these poems into your mind, your time, and your heart. May they offer you moments of reflection and connection, and may you find comfort and inspiration in the rhythm of these verses.

With gratitude and hope,

Sanvi Bhandari

1. Is it me ?

Is it me who gazes at the sky,

Or does the sky look down on me,

Pitying my path with its endless hues,

While my own palette appears so bleak?

Is it me who has made friends with shadows,

Or does my fear of the light recoil me?

Or perhaps it's my heart, pounding and scared,

Unwilling to show its wounds in the blinding glare?

Am I the one asking these questions,

Or is it my loneliness pondering aloud?

Is it answers that I yearn for,

Or merely the care I need?

Is it me or my curious mind wandering?

My heart, a restless steed,

Craves more of the thrill,

The aftertaste of adventure on its tongue.

Is it me seeking to break free from this cage,

Or my impatience with the restless nights,

Hoping for a purpose yet to be fulfilled?

I ask again: Is it truly me who questions,

Or a world pressing in,

Unaware of who I wish to become?

Is it me finding joy in the quest for identity,

Or my fear of how the world will judge me?

Believing time will pass eases my tears,

Yet calms my fears, making happiness seem
near.

All these questions weigh me down,

But the answers call me higher.

Still, the heaviest question remains:

What is the happiness I truly seek?

2. Shedded skin

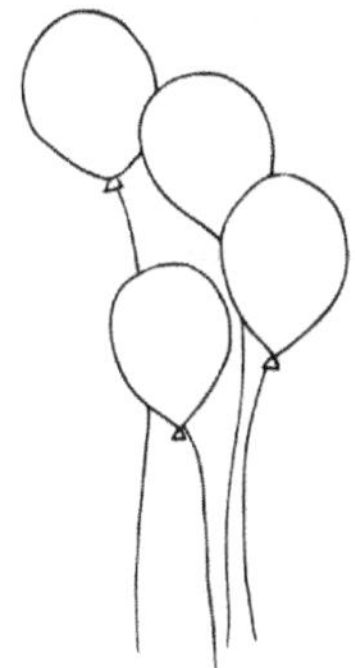

Did I lose you along the journey we embarked upon?

Or were you never there through my nights of struggle, trembling, shuddering, drowning in grief?

Oh, where did you go? I can no longer find you.

I search within myself for a laughing soul,

And every day I ask my teenage self: Will I ever be enough?

When bravery was my only choice,

Where were you to make me smile along the way?

Every tear that streaked my face,

Burned my skin and pierced my soul.

Yet, thanks to you, I emerged
stronger—stronger than ever.

Every scar became a star,

Every drop of that lustrous, opaque red fluid,

The essence of our existence, became an army
of thousands.

Every touch of pain that melted my bones,
and made me weaker,

Only served to make me rise again.

You lost, but we won.

You died, but we lived.

You left , but we stayed.

With your fragments left within me, perhaps I
will:

Learn to make my heart smile again,

Learn to wear my heart on my sleeve,

Learn to let go,

Learn to accept myself, mold myself with the
arrows and bullets the world gave me.

I hear your whispers within me, but I won't
let you take over—not anymore.

Is it too late for you to see?

You were the weak in me,

The leak within me, yet I still loved you,

Even though you weakened me.

3. The Material jungle

In the material jungle,

Oh, what a place to breathe—

Fresh, lush green-drenched dollar scents

Fill the air, a rich reprieve.

I wonder what unspoiled leaves smell like?

In the material jungle,

Oh, what a place to be me—

Like a mirror,

 Transparent is what I wish to be.

But those Tiffany diamonds gleam brighter;

When will it be time to tell myself,

"It's a pleasure to know you". . .

In the material jungle,

Oh, what a place to open my eyes!

Every day is different,

And everyone drifts with the tide.

I wonder what it feels like to be blind,

To see the true glitters shine.

In the material jungle,

I wonder what it means to be alive!

4. वह भी क्या ज़माना था

वह भी क्या ज़माना था,

जब वक़्त गुज़ारने के लिए दोस्तों से मिलने की
तलब थी,

और अब यह हाल है कि दोस्तों से मिलने के लिए
वक़्त की तलाश है।

वह भी क्या ज़माना था,

जब यारों को सरहदें भी रोक नहीं सकती थीं,

और आज एक काग़ज़ के पन्ने ने उन रिश्तों में दरार डाल दी है।

13

वह भी क्या ज़माना था।

५. दर्द से दोस्ती

टूटे थे हम भी कभी,

आँखें हमारी भी नम हुई थीं कभी,

दिल हमारा भी भटका था कभी,

नींद हमारी भी हुई थी बेवफ़ा।

ज़हर तो हमने भी चखा हैं लाखों बार,

फिर भी तुम पूछते हो, "क्या तुम्हें दर्द हुआ?"

अब हमने टूट के खुद को जोड़ना सीख लिया,

अपनी आँखों को खुद से पोंछना सीख लिया।

अपने दिल का रास्ता ढूँढ लिया,

लोरियों से नींद को भुलाना सीखा,

ज़हर को अपने हाथों से पीना सीख लिया,

तपती धूप से कर ली यारी।

हमने अपने दर्द को छुपाना नहीं, अपनाना सीख लिया,

अब खुद को संभालना सिख लिया।

6. To be that little girl again

The rustle of a chocolate wrapper,

The aroma of my mother's home-cooked feasts,

The rush of joy when my father returned from work—

These simple moments once sent happiness cascading through my veins.

But time has a way of rewriting our
memories.

The rustle of chocolate now reminds me of
calories,

My mother's cooking a rare indulgence,

And glimpses of my father, once vivid, now
phantoms in my mind.

Now, my eyes swell with a numb ache,

Shackled by the chains of society's
expectations,

I long for a Time Machine—

A chance to catch a glimpse of that little girl,

Unaware of the world's complications,

Untouched by its weight, most of all, happy
from within.

To see that little girl again,

Nestled safely in my father's arms,

Protected from the world's harsh bullets,

To feel the warmth of my mother's hand

Lulling me into dreamland each night.

Oh, what I would give to be that child once
more,

To reclaim that innocent joy,

To be that little girl again!

7. ज़िंदगी

वह वक़्त कैसा जिससे तुम रोक सको,

वह दर्द कैसा जो महसूस ना हो,

वह प्यार कैसा जो लहू से लाल ना हो,

वह ख़ुशी कैसी जब आँसुओं की क़ीमत पता ना
हो।

वह धूप कैसी जब बरसात ना हो,

वह अल्फ़ाज़ कैसे जिनमे आवाज़ ना हो,

वह ज़िंदगी कैसी जिसको जीने की आस ना हो।

8. Fear vs Failure

Fear has lost more battles than failure.

Fear holds us back, failure gives us wings.

Failure gives the ability to fall and to rise over and over again.

Fear creates regrets, while failure forges lessons from mistakes.

Fear is the past, but failures are just another step towards the future.

Fear is the armor we wear into battle, But failure is the courage we wear to be able to stand there.

Don't fear to fail—fail until fear fades!

9. In the realm of sound

The rhythm lifts me higher

As I yield to the sovereignty of my
headphones,

Letting music engulf me,

Shattering the deafening silence of my life.

The plethora of sounds weaves harmony,

Creating a world within society's confines.

A sanctuary where I can scream, cry, laugh, or
rejoice—

Even amidst my solitude, there's peace in that.

Music consumes me,

Yet it shields more than it endangers,

Empowering me to paint my world in hues of
sound.

In this sonic cage, I find a freedom unknown,

Meeting myself anew each day,

Crafting a new me without forsaking the real.

In this fantasy realm,

Where walls echo my thoughts,

Floors pulse with the beats I surrender to,

Flowers bloom to the symphony of my
emotions,

And the sky mirrors my soul—

It's a world where reality cannot harm.

I wish I could stay here forever,

But what's peace without a trace of chaos?

10. I am a girl

"Don't sit like that, you are a girl."

"Don't speak in that tone, you are a girl."

"Don't eat like that, you are a girl."

"What are you wearing? You are a girl."

These constant reminders of my existence—

What's their purpose?

I am lost in the echo of these voices,

Unaware of their true intent.

I know I am a girl.

I know my worth,

And I don't need their words to shape me

Into a person they want me to be.

I can be my own person,

Have my own voice,

Sit as I choose,

Speak the tone that I feel is right,

Eat as I please,

Wear what embodies my essence.

I am more than their expectations,

More than their constraints.

I am the sum of my choices,

The power of my self-discovery.

In my space, I write my own rules,

And I will not be caged

In their iron bars of their narrow visions.

I will embrace the fullness of who I am,

Unbound by their limitations.

Standing on the edge—ready to break free...

11. Home

These flawlessly painted white walls,

Impressively polished floors,

Exquisitely placed art pieces,

Perfectly plated meals,

Feather-like comforters,

The vast knowledge of books—

A perfect world will never come close to...

The contagious laughter of my sister,

The warm embrace of my father,

The comfort of my mother's lap,

The harmony in my grandmother's cooking,

The profound security in my grandfather's
wisdom,

The love from my family, the care from my
friends.

The friendly quarrels with my mother,

The loving fights with my sister—

It's these imperfect moments

That make life perfect.

12. Metropolitan symphony

A sniff of the metropolitan summer air,

With a lingering essence of monsoon breeze,

Towering concrete giants, standing tall and proud,

While the timid sky peeks through.

A city that forges harmony from chaos—

Bustling streets, deafening honks,

People scattered like tiny ants,

All blending into a perfectly curated
orchestra of nature.

Here, adrenaline flows where oxygen should,

Everyone dances to the rhythm of the chaos,

Existing in their own worlds but living the
same life.

A city that educates us,

Even when the sky is obscured by towers of
troubles,

Remember to dance in the sunlight,

Not to languish in the shadows.

13. A rainy night

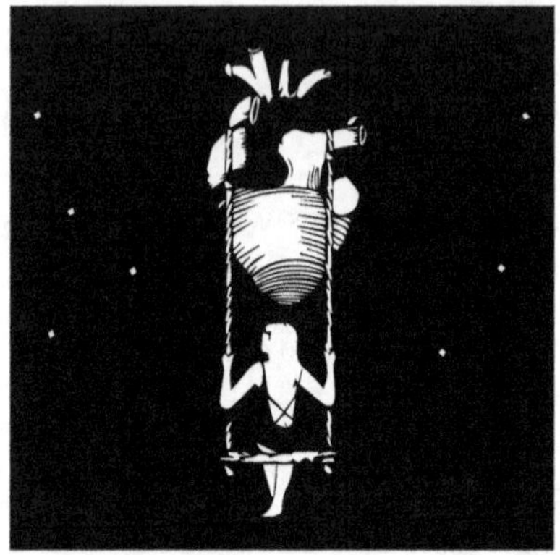

That drop of rain cradles the celestial night
sky

Within its delicate embrace,

While the misty breeze wraps around,

Hugging me gently.

Tears of the sky magnify, revealing true joys,

Emerald green grass illuminated,

Lightning streaks boldly like strands of white
gold in the sky.

The sky lets down its pitch-black hair,

Painting the day into night.

Lights grow brighter, objects seem dim,

Nature pulses with life—

Such is the power of night.

14. A comfort in the cold

The stiffness of the cold pierces like needles

On a weary winter morning.

Yet, the comfort of my sheets,

The warmth they offer,

Transforms those needles into feathers,

Cradling me like a child in her mother's arms.

When the world seems reluctant to wake,

The sun becomes lazy,

The wind turns merciless,

Grass glistens like shards of glass.

A little cranky, a little nice—

Like a child.

But the solace of a warm glass of turmeric
milk,

By the window,

Watching the world dawdle through time,

Reveals a world in transition,

Taking its time, not rushing through the
seasons.

A time both peaceful and slow,

With a touch of pain and a murmur of peace.

I found my comfort in the cold.

15. My Mumma

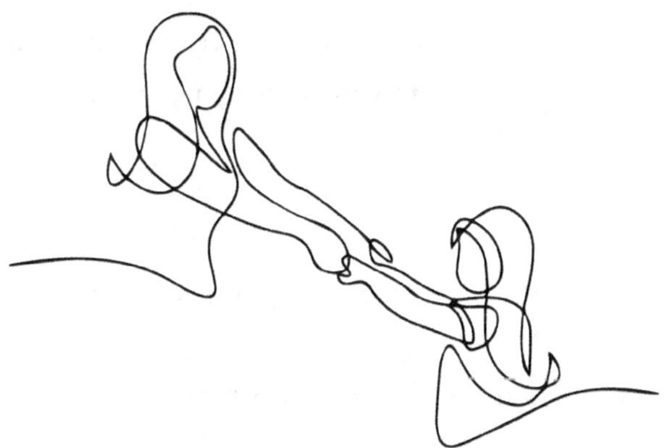

She carries the weight of three lives on her
back,

Lives not for herself,

Dreams of dreams that don't bear her name,

Paints skies that don't exist in her world.

She wakes each day so that others' days can
shine,

Claps silently, not for her own efforts, but for my achievements.

Shouts loudly, not to vent her frustration, but to guide my failures into my achievements.

She listens to both my joy and my sorrow,

Even when no one else hears her.

She speaks not for herself, but for me,

Making this life worth living.

Who is she?

My mumma.

16. My papa

I walked through the flood,

Not because you shielded me,

But because you taught me how

To stand tall and fight my own battles.

I stumbled and fell,

But I got up,

Not because you lifted me,

But because you showed me

How to rise.

When people mocked me,

I laughed,

Not because you defended me,

But because you taught me

The power of self-respect and dignity.

When others tried to bring me down,

I stood firm,

Not because you interceded,

But because you showed me

That my worth was never theirs to define.

When I felt sad,

You didn't come to comfort me,

But you taught me

To seek joy within myself.

Unlike others,

You didn't hand me everything,

But made me earn it,

To understand its value.

You taught me to be my own hero,

To be content with myself,

And to find pride in my own achievements.

You sacrificed everything for my smile,

And still felt it was not enough.

You carry countless burdens with a smile

To ensure mine never fades.

You built me a magnificent world

From the hardships you endured,

Just to see me happy.

I am proud of you, Papa.

17. My sister

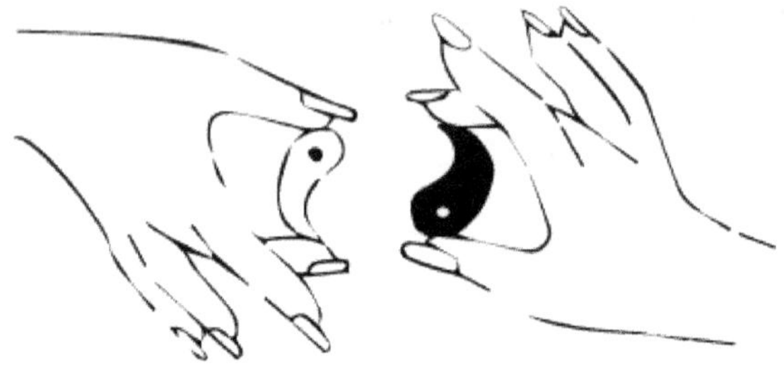

A person who wove her joy within mine,

Her sorrow within mine,

Her peace within mine,

Her childhood within mine,

Her teenage within mine.

When the world lies, she reveals the truth,

When the world laughs, she stands as my
shield,

When the world condemns, she offers praise.

45

She becomes

My shield,

My confidant,

No matter the time or place,

My best friend,

My sister.

18. The Shift

I wonder how we went from being mesmerized

By the colors of freshly bloomed flowers,

To being spellbound

By the vibrant pixels of the TV.

I wonder how we went from being thrilled

By the rush of talking to someone afar,

To continuously avoiding phone calls.

I wonder how we once rushed to our friends

With boundless enthusiasm,

Only to become reluctant

Even in replying to a simple text.

I wonder how we shifted

From being humans with humanity

To humans learning humanity.

19. Unfinished

An artist never truly finishes a painting,

But there comes a point where they must stop.

A dish is never quite complete,

Yet there are just enough ingredients to relish.

Some things are best left unfinished,

Like life—

It never has everything needed to live fully,

But it offers enough to make us smile.

20. ज़िंदा

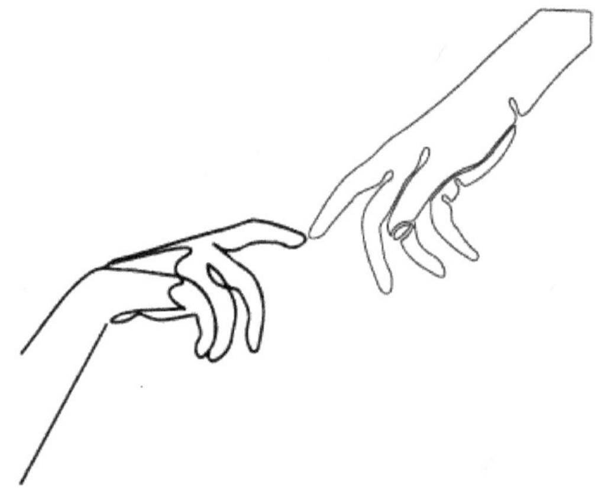

डूबने वाले के लिए एक तिनके का सहारा भी बहुत है,

प्यासे के लिए एक बूँद भी काफी है,

मरने वाले के लिए एक साँस भी बहुत है,

प्यार करने वाले के लिए एक लम्हा भी काफी है।

शायरी का मतलब तलाशा नहीं जाता,

शायरी तो वह रक़्स है, जिसमें

खुदको को पा कर भी खोने की चाह रहती है।

इन पैरों को रोक सको तो मानूँ,

अगर यह रुक गए तो वह कोसने जानता है,

जाना में कैसे जानूँ।

मौत का डर तो उन्हें होता है

जिन्हें जीने का ख़ौफ़ है।

जो ज़िंदा रहते सिर्फ़ ज़िंदा रहने के लिए,

वह कभी जी नहीं सकते।

और जो एक बार जी लेते हैं,

वह कभी सिर्फ़ ज़िंदा रहने के लिए नहीं जीना
चाहते।

52

21. Be you not them

Whoever is reading this,

Remember, you are undeniably you.

"You" can be unique,

"You" can be beautiful,

"You" can be strong.

You are the best version of yourself

That will ever exist.

Don't build yourself cages

From the jagged words the world throws at you.

Carve them into arrows,

Sharpen them with resilience,

Prepare to battle.

There will be days when you may not feel up for the fight.

People may say, "It's going to be okay."—

Lies, lies, lies.

It's obviously not.

Time is a strange thing.

It can pass in a second or linger on for
eternity.

You can't keep it, nor can you truly let it go,

But you can decide how you spend it.

Spend it by being you,

Not by becoming them.